A Walsingham Rosary

A Walsingham Rosary

Philip and Anne Gray

CANTERBURY
PRESS
Norwich

© Philip and Anne Gray, 2014

Published in 2014 by the Canterbury Press Norwich
Editorial office
3rd Floor, Invicta House,
108–114 Golden Lane,
London EC1Y 0TG

Published in 2000 by McCrimmon Publishing Co.

Canterbury Press is an imprint of Hymns Ancient & Modern Ltd
(a registered charity)
13A Hellesdon Park Road, Norwich,
Norfolk NR6 5DR, UK

www.canterburypress.co.uk

British Library Cataloguing in Publication data

A catalogue record for this book is available
from the British Library

978 1 84825 630 9

Typeset by Regent Typesetting
Printed and bound in Great Britain by
Ashford Colour Press, Gosport, Hants

CONTENTS

INTRODUCTION

Pilgrimage as a religious instinct has too often been supplanted by travel for its own sake, and the aim of this book is to encourage a spiritually motivated visit to various sites as a supplement to the usual Walsingham pilgrimage programme. It is also our intention to renew the Rosary devotion in an age which uses 'worry beads' to alleviate stress, but with no sacred purpose. The Rosary can be used for meditation, intercessory and penitential prayer, or a combination of all three.

This is the second edition of this book and now includes the five Luminous Mysteries, which reflect upon Our Lord's ministry and which the Church continues at His command. This book is purposely ecumenical in nature. As long ago as August 1895, Pope Leo XIII, who donated the statue of Our Lady to Kings Lynn in 1897, wrote:

> No doubt the many changes that have come about, and time itself, have caused the existing divisions to take deeper root. But is that a reason to give up all hope of remedy, reconciliation and peace? By no means if God is with us … care should be taken that prayers for unity already established among Catholics on certain fixed days should be made popular and recited with greater devotion, and especially the pious practice of the Holy Rosary, which we ourselves have so strongly recommended, should flourish, for it contains as it were a summary of the Gospel teaching and has always been a most salutary institution for the people at large.

In 1948 Fr Alfred Hope Patten, priest-restorer of the Anglican Shrine, wrote in the Pilgrims' Manual:

> Nearly ten years after the Anglican revival of the devotion to Our Lady of Walsingham the Roman Catholics adapted the Slipper Chapel at Houghton-in-the-Dale and formed it into their shrine and very large crowds of pilgrims visit it yearly. Our hope and prayer is that where there is such an evident common devotion to the Mother of Our Lord there will develop an overpowering desire for true Catholic reunion, and that through Our Lady's prayers, in God's good time, Anglican, Orthodox and Roman Catholics may find joy in complete internal and external unity.

The recently established Anglican Welcome Centre continues this vision:

> At Both Shrines we pray for the unity of the Church and for the day when there need only be one church in this holy domain.

May we always hold fast to the assurance of the angel Gabriel to Our Lady:

> Nothing is impossible for God.

We hope that this book will, in some small way, help all Christians to grow together into the unity for which Christ prayed, and also encourage visits to these hallowed places. We include the photographs or drawings for each site to enable people to pray these mysteries at home and transport themselves in spirit to these places 'where prayer has been valid'.

Philip and Anne Gray

THE ROSARY

The Rosary is a form of prayers and meditations said with the aid of a string of beads. The main circle is divided into five groups known as 'decades' – each having ten beads close together and one further apart. There is an additional short chain (or string) finishing at a Crucifix; this has two single beads separated by a group of three together.

Each decade is dedicated to one of the five 'Mysteries' of its group. There are four groups of five, and each completes one circuit of the Rosary. They are called:

The Joyful Mysteries

1   the Annunciation of Our Lord by Gabriel to Mary
2   the Visitation of Mary to Elizabeth
3   the Nativity of Our Lord
4   the Presentation of Our Lord in the Temple
5   the Finding of Our Lord in the Temple.

The Sorrowful Mysteries

1   the Agony in the Garden of Gethsemane
2   the Scourging of Our Lord
3   the Crowning with Thorns
4   the Carrying of the Cross
5   the Crucifixion.

The Luminous Mysteries

1   *the Baptism of Our Lord*
2   *the Marriage at Cana*
3   *the Proclamation of the Kingdom of God*
4   *the Transfiguration of Our Lord*
5   *the Institution of the Eucharist.*

The Glorious Mysteries

1   *the Resurrection*
2   *the Ascension of Our Lord*
3   *the Coming of the Holy Spirit*
4   *the Assumption of Mary into Heaven*
5   *the Coronation of Mary as Queen of Heaven.*

The Rosary has been described as 'the Bible translated into prayer'. As a means of meditation, it enables these mysteries to take root in our lives, it helps our spiritual horizons expand in praying for other people and their needs and it can deepen our penitence.

BEGINNING THE ROSARY

The purpose of the beads is to still our bodies and focus our minds on the mysteries. The words of the prayers set the tone and act rather like a mantra, or background music. We cease to concentrate on the repetitive prayer, but allow it to quieten us so that we are able to meditate. Rather than allowing ourselves to become distracted by other things, we are occupying our hands and our surface thoughts using the beads and the words of the prayers, which in turn channel our thoughts to the meditations. That is why we don't have to worry about concentrating on every word we are saying, but rather allow them all to sink into our subconscious minds.

The Short Chain

- The Rosary is commonly begun at the Crucifix, by making the sign of the Cross and reciting the Apostles' Creed.
- On the first single bead is said an 'Our Father' (the Lord's Prayer). Then follow three 'Hail Mary's on the group of three beads (usually one to God the Father who created her, one to God the Son who redeemed her and one to God the Holy Spirit who sanctified her).
- On the chain after this group of three is said a 'Glory be ...'

The Circle

- The Mystery for meditation is usually announced before each decade.
- We begin each decade on the first single bead (or the last one on the short chain) with an 'Our Father'.
- On each of the next ten beads we recite a 'Hail Mary', while allowing our minds to meditate on the particular Mystery.
- A 'Glory be …' is said on the chain to conclude that Mystery.

Using the Rosary Regularly

There is no virtue in 'doing it all at once', and it can be more beneficial to say one decade a day. It can then be recalled several times during the day and linked with the daily Mass readings.

One suggested use is to contemplate a different Mystery each day in succession.

Alternatively a whole decade can be prayed at a time as follows:

Sundays in Advent:	Joyful	Mondays:	Joyful
Sundays in Lent:	Sorrowful	Tuesdays:	Sorrowful
All other Sundays:	Glorious	Wednesday:	Glorious
		Thursdays:	Luminous
		Fridays:	Sorrowful
		Saturdays:	Joyful

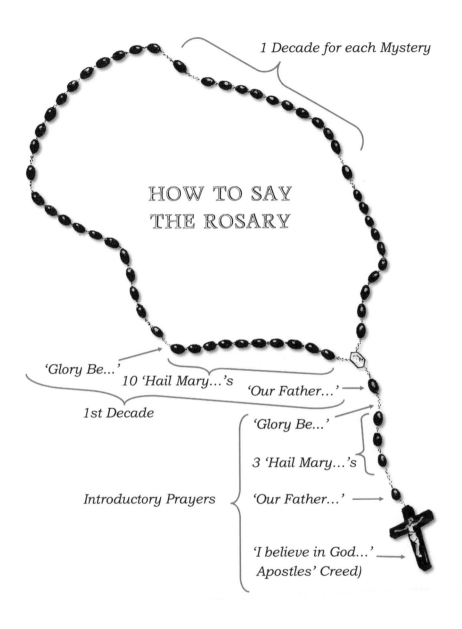

1 Decade for each Mystery

HOW TO SAY
THE ROSARY

'Glory Be...'

10 'Hail Mary...'s

'Our Father...'

1st Decade

'Glory Be...'

3 'Hail Mary...'s

Introductory Prayers

'Our Father...'

'I believe in God...'
Apostles' Creed)

THE PRAYERS

+ In the Name of the Father and of the Son and of the Holy Spirit. AMEN

The Apostles' Creed

I believe in God, the Father almighty,
Creator of heaven and earth.
I believe in Jesus Christ, His only Son, our Lord.
He was conceived by the power of the Holy Spirit and born of the
    Virgin Mary.
He suffered under Pontius Pilate, was crucified, died and was buried.
He descended to the dead.
On the third day He rose again.
He ascended into heaven,
and is seated at the right hand of the Father.
He will come again to judge the living and the dead.
I believe in the Holy Spirit,
the holy catholic Church,
the communion of saints,
the forgiveness of sins,
the resurrection of the body and life everlasting.
AMEN

OR

I believe in God, the Father Almighty, maker of Heaven and earth,
And in Jesus Christ, His only Son, Our Lord,
Who was conceived by the Holy Spirit,
Born of the Virgin Mary,
Suffered under Pontius Pilate,
Was crucified, dead and buried.
He descended into Hell.
The third day He rose again.
He ascended into Heaven
And is seated at the right hand of God,
the Father Almighty,
From whence He shall come to judge
the quick and the dead.
I believe in the Holy Ghost,
The Holy Catholick Church,
The Communion of Saints,
The forgiveness of sins,
The resurrection of the body
And the life everlasting.
AMEN

Our Father

Our Father, Who art in Heaven, hallowed be Thy name.
Thy kingdom come;
Thy will be done on earth as it is in heaven.
Give us this day our daily bread;
And forgive us our trespasses as we forgive those who trespass
    against us.
And lead us not into temptation:
But deliver us from evil. AMEN

Hail Mary

Hail Mary, full of grace, the Lord is with thee;
Blessed art thou amongst women and blessed is the fruit of thy
    womb, Jesus.
Holy Mary, Mother of God, pray for us sinners now
And at the hour of our death. AMEN

Glory be

Glory be to the Father and to the Son and to the Holy Spirit;
As it was in the beginning, is now and ever shall be, world without
    end. AMEN

THE JOYFUL MYSTERIES

THE JOYFUL MYSTERIES

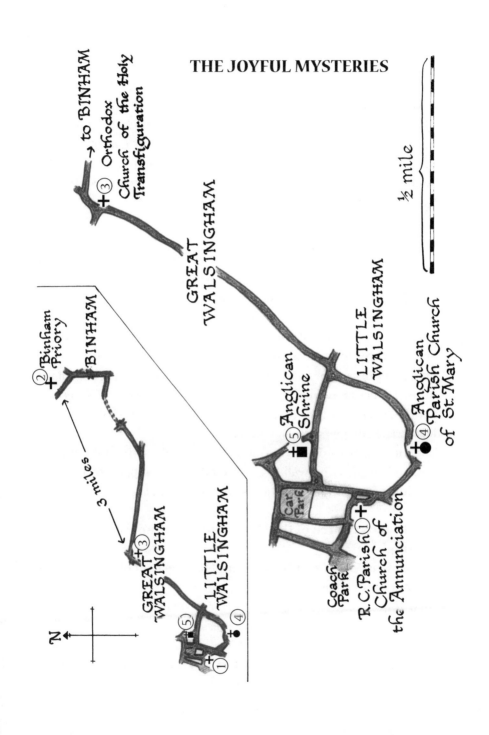

½ mile

to BINHAM →

③ + Orthodox Church of the Holy Transfiguration

GREAT WALSINGHAM

② + Binham Priory

BINHAM

③ + GREAT WALSINGHAM

3 miles

LITTLE WALSINGHAM

④ +●

⑤ + ■

① +

N

⑤ + ■ Anglican Shrine

Car Park

LITTLE WALSINGHAM

Coach Park

① + R.C. Parish Church of the Annunciation

④ + ● Anglican Parish Church of St Mary

DIRECTIONS

1 RC Church of the Annunciation

The RC Parish Church of the Annunciation, Walsingham, is in Friday Market, between the Black Lion and the Roman Catholic Pilgrim Bureau. Refreshments are available at the Black Lion.

(Methodist Chapel: optional detour – see travel directions after the First Joyful Mystery, page 9)

2 Binham Priory

Turn **left** onto the High Street, then **right** by the Pump, passing the Anglican Shrine and Knight Street on your left. After about 200 yards turn **left** into Scarborough Road, signed *Great Walsingham ½, Binham 3½ and Orthodox Church.*

Continue through Great Walsingham and remain on the same road for another three miles until you reach Binham. (There is a lovely view of Binham Priory on the left about half a mile before reaching the village.) At the T-junction turn **left**; a brown tourist sign marks *Binham Priory*.

Continue through the village for about a quarter of a mile and turn **left** by the Chequers Inn, signed *Warham 3*.

The entrance to the Priory is a few hundred yards on the **right** and well signed through a flint wall. There is ample space for parking. There are also toilet facilities. Refreshments are available at the Chequers Inn.

3 Orthodox Church of the Holy Transfiguration, Great Walsingham

Retrace journey to Great Walsingham. (Turn **left** out of the Priory and **right** at the Chequers Inn.)

Take the second turning **right** after a quarter of a mile, signed *Walsingham*, and continue for three miles.

At Great Walsingham, after Great Walsingham Gallery on the right, the road turns sharp **left**. The Orthodox Church is just after this on the **left**, opposite a road signed *Unbridged Ford*. Park either outside the church, or alongside the Green opposite. Refreshments are available in the Walsingham Café, by Great Walsingham Gallery.

4 St Mary's Church, Little Walsingham
Continue along Scarborough Road, past the Orthodox Church on your left, towards Little Walsingham.

At the cross roads, cross **diagonally** (with care!) and continue about 300 yards to St Mary's.

Park either in the lane alongside the churchyard wall or in the space in front of the church.

5 Anglican Shrine of Our Lady of Walsingham
Continue along Church Street, with St Mary's Church behind you.

Turn **right** at the junction into the High Street, turning **left** by the Pump to park in the car park. Walk back past the Shrine Shop through the Common Place. The entrance to the Anglican Shrine is on the **left** after the Welcome Centre. Enter through the brick archway. Refreshments are available in the Norton's Café Bar in the Anglican Shrine grounds.

First Joyful Mystery

THE ANNUNCIATION OF OUR LORD
Said at the Church of the Annunciation, Friday Market

Roman Catholic Church of the Annunciation.

This Roman Catholic Church, built in 2006, is on the site of the previous church built in 1950. It contains a copy of the statue of Our Lady in the Church of the Annunciation, Kings Lynn, given by Pope Leo XIII in 1897, when devotion to Our Lady of Walsingham was first revived. This statue was given by the Guild of Our Lady of Ransom, which has been among Walsingham's keenest supporters ever since. The statue was based on a picture in the Church of St Maria in Cosmedia in Rome. This was the titular church of Cardinal Reginald Pole, the last Archbishop of Canterbury to be in communion with the See of Peter, and hence was considered appropriate for the statue of Our Lady of Walsingham.

GOSPEL   Luke 1.26–38

The angel Gabriel was sent by God to a town in Galilee called Nazareth, to a virgin betrothed to a man named Joseph, of the House of David, and the virgin's name was Mary. He went in and said to her, 'Rejoice, so highly favoured! The Lord is with you.' She was deeply disturbed by these words and asked herself what this greeting could mean, but the angel said to her, 'Mary, do not be afraid; you have won God's favour. Listen! You are to conceive and bear a son, and you must name him Jesus. He will be great and will be called Son of the Most High. The Lord God will give him the throne of his ancestor David; he will rule over the House of Jacob for ever and his reign will have no end.' Mary said to the angel, 'But how can this come about, since I am a virgin?' 'The Holy Spirit will come upon you,' the angel answered. 'And the power of the Most High will cover you with its shadow. And so the child will be holy and will be called Son of God. Know this too: your kinswoman Elizabeth has, in her old age, herself conceived a son, and she whom people called barren is now in her sixth month, for nothing is impossible to God.' 'I am the handmaid of the Lord,' said Mary, 'let what you have said be done to me.' And the angel left her.

This is the Gospel of the Lord.

PAUSE

ACT OF PENITENCE

Forgive us, Lord, when we say 'No' to you. Lord have Mercy.
All   Lord have mercy.

Forgive us, Lord, for not taking up the challenge before us. Christ have mercy.
All   Christ have mercy.

Forgive us, Lord, when we do not rely on you through the power of the Holy Spirit. Lord have mercy.
All   Lord have mercy.

*Statue of Our Lady
in the Church of the
Annunciation.*

INTERCESSIONS

Let us pray for all Christians, that we may listen carefully to God's call and act according to His will as Mary did.

Let us pray for all expectant mothers, that they may treasure the children they carry with love and joy.

Let us pray for all who are called to bear the burden of authority, the glare of public life or who are entrusted with great artistic or sporting talents.

We pray for all who care for the disabled and those with learning difficulties; that they may be given strength in their special responsibilities.

Let us pray for those who have never heard God's call; for those who refuse to hear it; for those who set out and turn back and for those who, without question, answer it.

Father, we pray for those who work for the reunion of all Christians. May we constantly pray for a new heart and a new spirit, so we may build bridges that unite rather than barriers that divide.

All **Mary, teach me, too, to say 'Yes',**
I am the handmaid of the Lord;
Let all He wills be done in me.
May His Spirit overshadow me,
His love be fruitful in me,
His joy abound in my heart.
Let there be no 'Yes, but …'
Which is really a cover for 'No'.
Let it all be 'Yes', plain and simple,
A 'Yes', spoken in trust to the One who is eternally faithful.
AMEN

Let us now consider God sending an angel to Mary. Mary said, 'Yes', to God; her 'Yes' was total and she was overshadowed by the Holy Spirit.

We pray this Mystery that we may open our hearts to the Holy Spirit, that God may make His home in us and that we may be servants of God.

Our Father …

———————

*At this point is the option of a short detour to the Methodist Chapel to pray for unity. Turn **right** from the Church of the Annunciation, past the RC Pilgrim Bureau to the end. The chapel stands back from the road in the space after the brick and flint beamed house. It is a particularly fine red brick building dating from 1794. John Wesley had preached in Walsingham in 1781 and lamented the destruction of the Shrine. The chapel is open from Whitsun to the end of October on Thursdays, Fridays, Saturdays and Bank Holidays from 2.00 pm to 4.30 pm. Whether or not it is open, we can offer a prayer for the unity of all Christians, including our non-conformist brothers and sisters, who share our common Baptism. 'May they all be one, Father, may they be one in us, as you are in me and I am in you, so that the world may believe …'(John 17.21).*

Second Joyful Mystery

THE VISITATION OF MARY TO ELIZABETH

Said at Binham Priory – if weather permits
before the High Altar in the ruins

Binham was founded for Benedictine Monks in 1091 by Peter de Valoines, nephew of the Conqueror. The Priory was dissolved in 1540, the nave becoming the parish church. It is an evocative place for prayer, and a wonderful location for enjoying Norman and Early English architecture.

GOSPEL   Luke 1.39–56

Mary set out and went as quickly as she could to a town in the hill country of Judah. She went to Zechariah's house and greeted Elizabeth. Now as soon as Elizabeth heard Mary's greeting, the child leapt in her womb and Elizabeth was filled with the Holy Spirit. She gave a loud cry and said, 'Of all women you are the most blessed, and blessed is the fruit of your womb. Why should I be honoured with a visit from the mother of my Lord? For the moment your greeting reached my ears, the child in my womb leapt for joy. Yes, blessed is she who believed that the promise made her by the Lord would be fulfilled.'

And Mary said: 'My soul proclaims the greatness of the Lord and my spirit exults in God my saviour: because he has looked upon his lowly handmaid. Yes, from this day forward all generations will call me blessed, for the Almighty has done great things for me. Holy is his name; and his mercy reaches from age to age for those who fear him. He has shown the power of his arm, he has routed the proud of heart. He has pulled down princes from their thrones and exalted the lowly. The hungry he has filled with good things, the rich sent empty away. He has come to the help of Israel his servant, mindful of his mercy – according to the promise he made to our ancestors – of his mercy to Abraham and to his descendants for ever.'

This is the Gospel of the Lord.

PAUSE

Priory Church of St Mary and the Holy Cross.

ACT OF PENITENCE

Forgive us, Lord, for our lack of warmth in relationships. Lord have mercy.

All   Lord have mercy.

Forgive us, Lord, when we fail to recognize your Spirit in each other. Christ have mercy.

All   Christ have mercy.

Forgive us, Lord, when we fail to recognise each person as our neighbour. Lord have mercy.

All   Lord have mercy

INTERCESSIONS

By the light of the Holy Spirit, Elizabeth knew that Jesus was in Mary. Like Elizabeth, may we, too, see Christ in our neighbour.

Let us pray that we may respond immediately and unselfishly to the needs of others. We pray especially for those who provide hospitality for travellers and those who take care of mothers and babies.

Let us pray for all who, like Zechariah, doubt God's wisdom and power. May we join with Mary in saying; 'The Almighty has done great things for me.'

Mary went with haste to Elizabeth; may we respond eagerly to the Holy Spirit in our lives.

Mary's Magnificat is a celebration of God's work in her; may we celebrate the gifts of God which we and others have received.

All **O Mary, you are a mystery of faithfulness, of light, of perfection. I love to think of you as bearer of Christ for others. Every child is for God and for others. I feel compelled as I carry Christ to others to remain in the background like you, so that only He may be seen. I am not running away or being detached, but I am lending Him my voice, my face, my life, my environment, so that through me He may speak and save and love all people today. AMEN**

Let us meditate on Mary's spirit of generosity in serving Christ by caring for other people. Elizabeth knew that Jesus was in Mary. The way we treat others is the way we love God, so may we see Christ in those we meet today. We pray this Mystery for the sick and all who care for them.

Our Father ...

PRAYER FOR ALL BENEDICTINES

God our Father,
You made St Benedict an outstanding guide
To teach us how to live in your service.
Grant that by preferring your love to everything else,
We may walk in the way of your commandments.
We ask this through Our Lord Jesus Christ, Your Son,
Who lives and reigns with you and the Holy Spirit,
One God, for ever and ever. AMEN

Third Joyful Mystery

THE NATIVITY OF OUR LORD

Said in the Orthodox Church of the Holy Transfiguration,
Great Walsingham

The Victorian Methodist Chapel by the Village Green was built in 1895 and converted into the Russian Orthodox Church of the Holy Transfiguration in 1988. The icons adorning the interior are painted by members of the Brotherhood of St Seraphim.

GOSPEL   Luke 2.1–14

Now at this time Caesar Augustus issued a decree for a census of the whole world to be taken. This census – the first – took place while Quirinius was governor of Syria, and everyone went to his own town to be registered. So Joseph set out from the town of Nazareth to Galilee and travelled up to Judaea, to the town of David called Bethlehem, since he was of David's House and line, in order to be registered together with Mary, his betrothed, who was with child. While they were there the time came for her to have her child, and she gave birth to a son, her first-born. She wrapped him in swaddling clothes, and laid him in a manger because there was no room for them at the inn. In the countryside close by there were shepherds who lived in the fields and took it in turns to watch their flocks during the night. The angel of the Lord appeared to them and the glory of the Lord shone round them. They were terrified, but the angel said: 'Do not be afraid. Listen, I bring you news of great joy, a joy to be shared by the whole people. Today in the town of David a saviour has been born for you; he is Christ the Lord. And here is a sign for you: you will find a baby wrapped in swaddling clothes and lying in a manger.' And suddenly with the angel there was a great throng of the heavenly host, praising God and singing: 'Glory to God in the highest heaven, and peace to men who enjoy his favour.'

This is the Gospel of the Lord.

PAUSE

ACT OF PENITENCE

In Your birth, Lord, you have revealed God's unconditional love. Forgive us when we have responded half-heartedly. Lord have mercy.
All   Lord have mercy.

To all who accept you, Lord, you give power to become children of God. Forgive our lukewarm response. Christ have mercy.
All   Christ have mercy.

Forgive us, Lord, when we try to save ourselves without your help; when we have preferred darkness and failed to be true reflections of you. Lord have mercy.
All   Lord have mercy

*Detail of the Feast ikon in the Orthodox
Church of the Holy Transfiguration.*

INTERCESSIONS

Let us pray for ourselves; that we may welcome Christ into our lives with the simplicity of Mary, Joseph and the shepherds.

Father, may our hearts not be overcrowded with worldly concerns. May we glorify you as the shepherds did, and persevere as the Magi did.

We pray for all women who are giving birth and for all Christian parents; that the Lord may guide them in bringing up their children.

Let us pray that we may open our hearts to welcome Jesus however He wants to come to us.

We pray for Eastern and Western Christians sharing a common devotion to the Mother of God.

All **Jesus, living in Mary, come and live in us, your servants**
in the spirit of your holiness, in the fullness of your power,
in the reality of your virtues, in the perfection of your ways,
in the communication of your mysteries;
And by your Spirit conquer every adverse power.
To the Glory of God the Father. AMEN

SILENCE as we meditate upon the Orthodox Kontakion:

Today the Virgin bears Him beyond substance, and the earth offers a cave to the unapproachable. Angels with shepherds give glory. Wise men journey with the star: for He has been born for us.

We pray this Mystery for all families, particularly those living in poverty and for children born today.

Our Father ...

Fourth Joyful Mystery

THE PRESENTATION OF OUR LORD IN THE TEMPLE

Said in the Guilds Chapel of St Mary's, Little Walsingham

St Mary's Church.

This Church is built on the original Saxon site that Richeldis and her son, Geoffrey de Faverches, would have known. In the Guilds Chapel (north side of the chancel) Fr Alfred Hope Patten first set up a statue of Our Lady of Walsingham on 6 July 1922. The statue, copied from the mediaeval seal of Walsingham Priory, is now in the Holy House in the Anglican Shrine, while here in St Mary's is a small replica of Our Lady on the pillar looking towards the Priory grounds.

GOSPEL   Luke 2.22–40

And when the day came for them to be purified as laid down by the Law of Moses, they took him up to Jerusalem to present him to the Lord – observing what stands written in the Law of the Lord: Every first-born male must be consecrated to the Lord – and also to offer in sacrifice, in accordance with what is said in the Law of the Lord, a pair of turtledoves or two young pigeons. Now in Jerusalem there was a man named Simeon. He was an upright and devout man; he looked forward to Israel's comforting and the Holy Spirit rested on him. It had been revealed to him by the Holy Spirit that he would not see death until he had set eyes on the Christ of the Lord. Prompted by the Spirit he came to the Temple; and when the parents brought in the child Jesus to do for him what the Law required, he took him into his arms and blessed God: and he said: 'Now, Master, you can let your servant go in peace, just as you promised; because my eyes have seen the salvation which you have prepared for all the nations to see, a light to enlighten the pagans and the glory of your people Israel.'

As the child's father and mother stood there wondering at the things that were being said about him, Simeon blessed them and said to Mary his mother, 'You see this child; he is destined for the fall and for the rising of many in Israel, destined to be a sign that is rejected – and a sword will pierce your own soul too – so that the secret thoughts of many may be laid bare.'

There was a prophetess also, Anna, the daughter of Phanuel, of the tribe of Asher. She was well on in years. Her days of girlhood over, she had been married for seven years before becoming a widow. She was now eighty-four years old and never left the Temple, serving God night and day with fasting and prayer. She came by just at that moment and began to praise God; and she spoke of the child to all who looked forward to the deliverance of Jerusalem.

When they had done everything the Law of the Lord required, they went back to Galilee, to their own town of Nazareth. Meanwhile the child grew to maturity, and he was filled with wisdom; and God's favour was with him.

This is the Gospel of the Lord.

PAUSE

ACT OF PENITENCE

Forgive us, Lord, for the times we have been satisfied with any light but the light of Christ. Lord, have mercy.

All   Lord have mercy.

Forgive us, Lord, when we are in darkness and fail to pray for your light. Christ have mercy.

All   Christ have mercy.

Forgive us, Lord, when we fail to carry your light to all people. Lord have mercy.

All   Lord have mercy

Statue of Our Lady of Walsingham in the Guilds Chapel, St Mary's Church, site of Fr Alfred Hope Patten's first restored statue.

INTERCESSIONS

Let us pray for renewal of the Church's mission and for our parishes. May we be lights to all who live in the darkness of unbelief, and show the way to life in Christ.

We pray for all parents, especially for those in difficulties. May they model themselves on Joseph and Mary, who brought Christ to the Temple and lead their children to follow Christ.

Lord, we pray for the elderly; may they be like Simeon and Anna, whose lives were imbued with dedication, expectancy and prayer.

Mary was given a bitter prophecy by Simeon. We pray for all recipients of bad news, either for themselves or their loved ones. May they face the future with confidence in God as Mary did.

Father, we pray for ourselves; that we may witness the love of Jesus to everyone as Anna did.

All   Mary, our Mother, you consented in faith to become the mother of Jesus. At the angel's announcement you received the Word of God in your heart as well as in your body, and you brought life to the world. You conceived in your heart, with your whole being, before you conceived in your womb. Pray that we may have a faith similar to your own, which will enable us to hear the Word of God and carry it out. Let us imitate your motherhood by our faith, bringing Christ to birth in ourselves and others who have desperate need of Him. AMEN

Let us now consider Mary and Joseph making an offering to God of their newborn baby, who is God Himself. Let us pray that every thought, word and activity in our lives may be a presentation to God. May we witness the love of Jesus to all we meet, just as Simeon did in the temple.

We pray this Mystery for our parishes and congregations.

Our Father ...

At the grave of Fr Alfred Hope Patten (north of tower entrance)
Father of mercy,
You gave Alfred Hope Patten vision and strength
To restore the Holy House of the Shrine
Of Our Lady of Walsingham;
Make us, your pilgrim people,
Witnesses to the truth of the Incarnation,
That in word and action we may bring glory to your name,
Through Jesus Christ Your Son, our Lord, who is alive and reigns
     with you
In the unity of the Holy Spirit, One God, now and for ever. AMEN

Fifth Joyful Mystery

THE FINDING OF OUR LORD IN THE TEMPLE

Said in the Chapel dedicated to this Mystery in the Anglican Shrine
Church, dedicated in honour of St Thomas à Becket and St Philip Neri

Anglican Shrine Church.

*The Anglican Shrine Church was built between 1931 and 1937 – the inspiration
of Fr Alfred Hope Patten. The Holy House of Our Lady of Walsingham was re-
built according to the measurements of the original, as recorded by William of
Worcester, and many ancient stones from other churches, abbeys and shrines
were incorporated in the walls and altars. When the foundations were laid a
well was revealed beneath the Holy House dating from mediaeval times. This
Holy Well, fed by a natural spring, is a focal point of pilgrimage, and every*

pilgrim is invited to receive this Walsingham Water. The Shrine Church is constructed over the Holy House and has 15 chapels, each dedicated to a different Mystery of the Rosary.

To find the chapel of the Finding of Our Lord in the Temple: face the High Altar with your back to the Holy House. The chapel is the second on your right. Alongside it is a recumbent figure of Fr Arthur Tooth, imprisoned for refusing to obey the Public Worship Regulation Act of 1874 to suppress the growth of Ritualism in the Church of England. Under the altar in a decorated feretory are relics of St Thomas Becket. This chapel is now designated a chapel of prayer for young people.

––––––––––––

GOSPEL   Luke 2.41–52

Every year the parents of Jesus used to go to Jerusalem for the feast of the Passover. When he was twelve years old, they went up for the feast as usual. When they were on their way home after the feast, the boy Jesus stayed behind in Jerusalem without his parents knowing it. They assumed he was with the caravan, and it was only after a day's journey that they went to look for him among their relations and acquaintances. When they failed to find him they went back to Jerusalem looking for him everywhere.

Three days later, they found him in the Temple, sitting among the doctors, listening to them and asking them questions; and all those who heard him were astounded at his intelligence and his replies. They were overcome when they saw him, and his mother said to him, 'My child, why have you done this to us? See how worried your father and I have been, looking for you.' 'Why were you looking for me?' he replied. 'Did you not know that I must be busy with my Father's affairs?' But they did not understand what he meant.

He then went down with them and came to Nazareth and lived under their authority. His mother stored up all these things in her heart. And Jesus increased in wisdom, in stature and in favour with God and men.

This is the Gospel of the Lord.

PAUSE

ACT OF PENITENCE

Forgive us, Lord, when we refuse your forgiveness by not returning to you with our whole heart. Lord have mercy.

All   Lord have mercy

Forgive us, Lord, when we refuse to open our hearts to those we have injured and those who have injured us. Christ have mercy.

All   Christ have mercy

Forgive us, Lord, when we have allowed ourselves to be overpowered by our sinfulness. Lord have mercy.

All   Lord have mercy

Painting in the Chapel of the Finding of Our Lord in the Temple in the Anglican Shrine.

INTERCESSIONS

Let us pray for all children and young people; for all who serve at the altar; for all who are asking questions and those who have the responsibility of answering them.

Father, we pray for all children who are neglected or abused, for those who have disabilities and those who are terminally ill; may we treasure each child and remember they are all created in your image.

Lord, we pray for all who are tempted to give up their searching.

Let us pray for all women and men who have suffered heartbreak from abortions. For all who mourn their lost unborn children. May they be befriended by Christians who are able to show the compassion of Jesus.

We pray for all parents who have lost their children; for all who have taken their searching and sorrowing into God's house; for all whose confidence is severely shaken when things have gone wrong.

Father, we pray for those who have lost children in accidents or through the violence of others, that even in the midst of their grief, anger and despair they may find peace and comfort in you.

All   **Lord, send your blessing upon the young people of our world,**
and protect them from the false shepherds of this passing age.
Give to them a gift of discernment and the gift of faith, that
like your Son, they may increase in wisdom and in stature
and in favour with you and with all humankind.
To your Church, and all who would seek an influence in their lives,
give a profound sense of love and respect
and a renewed desire to serve and encourage the young
as they live the great adventure,
which is the very gift entrusted to us all.
We ask our prayer through Jesus Christ our Lord. AMEN

Let us consider the losing of Jesus and pray that we may search for Him to experience His love and share it with others. May we learn to recognise God's will by listening as Jesus did.

We pray this Mystery for all children and young people and those who care for them.

Our Father …

THE LUMINOUS MYSTERIES

THE LUMINOUS MYSTERIES

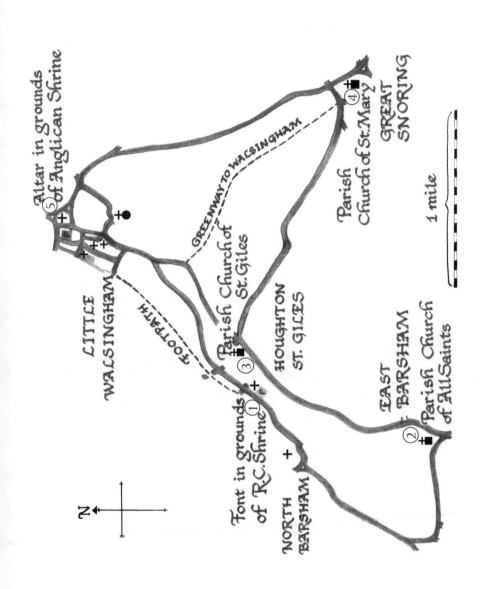

DIRECTIONS

1 RC National Shrine: Fountain in Cloister

Follow the signs to the Slipper Chapel, one mile south of Walsingham, leaving the village by the High Street towards Fakenham (passing the Friary ruins and lane to the coach park on your right). Turn next **right** towards the RC Shrine, signed *N&W Barsham, Slipper Chapel and Shrine*, where the road bends left for Fakenham. There is plenty of parking to the south of the Chapel of Reconciliation. Walk through the grounds, past the chapel entrance and the semicircle of crosses. The fountain is in the middle of the cloister near the bookshop. Refreshments are available at the RC Shrine.

2 All Saints' Church, East Barsham

Turn **left** out of the car park, going past abutments of a disused railway bridge (see North Barsham Church on your right). Turn **left** at the T-junction at the end of the grass triangle, signed *W Barsham/Fakenham*. After half a mile, in trees, turn **left**, signed *E Barsham 1*, and continue along the narrow road. East Barsham Church is at the top of the hill on the left before the T-junction. A few cars can park opposite the church on the grass on the right under the trees. (There is further parking by the White Horse, to the left of the T-junction.) Refreshments are available at the White Horse.

3 St Giles Church, Houghton St Giles

Turn **left**, at the T-junction, signed *Walsingham 2*, continuing past the White Horse and East Barsham Manor for just over a mile. Houghton St Giles Church is ahead on your left, just after a track on the left to an unbridged ford. You can park on the left before the church in the recess outside the churchyard.

4 St Mary's Church, Great Snoring

Continue along the road for a few yards, turning **right** at the first crossroads, signed *Gt Snoring*, and continue for about two miles. At the T-junction (facing red brick house) turn **right** into The Street, continue for a few yards beyond the postbox and park in the road opposite Great Snoring Church.

5 Altar of the Luminous Mysteries, Anglican Shrine

You now need to turn around to return to Walsingham, so continue for a few yards and make a U-turn **clockwise** around the grass triangle, taking the far **right** turning, signed *Fakenham 3*, then immediately turn **right** again, and turn **left** into The Street to re-pass Great Snoring Church on your left. Continue for two miles, pass the Anglican Shrine on your right and continue to the car park beyond the Pump (signed) or to Friday Market. Walk back to the Anglican Shrine through the red brick archway by the Welcome Centre. Continue ahead, following the path around the 'Hill of Calvary' to the outside altar. Refreshments are available in the Norton's Café Bar in the Anglican Shrine grounds.

THE BAPTISM OF OUR LORD

Said by the fountain in the Cloister behind the
Slipper Chapel, RC National Shrine

The font came from the medi-
aeval Parish Church of Forncett
St Mary, Norfolk, in 1981 during
the time it was redundant. The
surrounding panels are by Jane
Quail and depict:

- *The Good Shepherd (He leads*
  me by restful waters, Psalm
  23.22).
- *The Baptism of Jesus, with*
  Greek text of Luke 3.22 (This is
  my beloved Son).
- *The woman whom Jesus met*
  at the well (I will give you living
  water, John 6.14).
- *Moses at the Red Sea (Exodus*
  15.19).

Fountain in the cloister of the Roman
Catholic National Shrine, behind the
Slipper Chapel.

GOSPEL   Luke 3.15–16, 21–22

A feeling of expectancy had grown among the people, who were beginning to think that John might be the Christ, so John declared before
them all, 'I baptise you with water, but someone is coming, someone
who is more powerful than I am and I am not fit to undo the strap of
his sandals; he will baptise you with the Holy Spirit and fire.'

Now when all the people had been baptised and while Jesus after his
own baptism was at prayer, heaven opened and the Holy Spirit descended on him in bodily shape, like a dove. And a voice came from
heaven, 'You are my Son, the Beloved; my favour rests on you.'

This is the Gospel of the Lord.

PAUSE

ACT OF PENITENCE

Forgive us for the times when we have failed to be servants of God.
Lord have mercy.
All   Lord have mercy.

Forgive us for the times when we have preferred darkness to light.
Christ have mercy.
All   Christ have mercy.

Forgive us, Lord, for the times when we have failed to be open to the
Holy Spirit. Lord have mercy.
All   Lord have mercy.

INTERCESSIONS

Father, you empowered Jesus with the Holy Spirit for His ministry. Renew us with your Holy Spirit so we can better reveal Him at work in our lives.

We pray for all Christians: that we may live up to the call we received at Baptism to follow Christ.

We give thanks, Lord, for our own baptism and for those who helped to bring us to faith.

Let us pray for Godparents and Sponsors: may their example help all who are baptised to follow Christ.

May all Christians who share a common baptism be united in the one Body of Christ so that there can be an end to factions and discord.

All   Dear Mary, pray for me as I renew my Baptismal promises. May I seek to be what you are – obedient to God and overshadowed by the Holy Spirit.
AMEN

As we meditate on the Baptism of Jesus, when He was empowered by the Holy Spirit to carry out His ministry, let us remember that we, the members of His body, the Church, share in the same ministry. We pray for greater faithfulness in bringing the power of Christ to the world.

We offer this Mystery for the renewal of our Baptismal commitment.

Our Father ...

Second Luminous Mystery

THE MARRIAGE AT CANA

Said in All Saints' Church, East Barsham

All Saints' Church.

All Saints, East Barsham, is a 'sermon in stone'. Henry VIII stayed at the neighbouring East Barsham Manor before walking barefoot to the Shrine at Walsingham to pray for a male heir, and probably attended Mass in this church. If the seed of the split with Rome was sown here, we must trust that seeds of unity will be planted here at this centre of reparation and healing for our wounded past. The ruined chantry chapel (south side) and the broken altar stone in the chancel show the scars of the Reformation, but the newly restored Shrine of Our Lady of Greeting encourages us to pray for unity: 'Do whatever He tells you.'

GOSPEL   John 2.1–11

There was a wedding at Cana in Galilee. The mother of Jesus was there, and Jesus and his disciples had also been invited. When they ran out of wine, since the wine provided for the wedding was all finished, the mother of Jesus said to him, 'They have no wine.' Jesus said, 'Woman, why turn to me? My hour has not come yet.' His mother said to the servants, 'Do whatever he tells you.' There were six stone water jars standing there, meant for the ablutions that are customary among the Jews; each could hold twenty or thirty gallons. Jesus said to the servants, 'Fill the jars with water,' and they filled them to the brim. 'Draw some out now,' he told them, 'and take it to the steward.' They did this; the steward tasted the water, and it had turned into wine. Having no idea where it came from – only the servants who had drawn the water knew – the steward called the bridegroom and said, 'People generally serve the best wine first, and keep the cheaper sort till the guests have had plenty to drink; but you have kept the best wine till now.' This was the first of the signs given by Jesus: it was given at Cana in Galilee. He let his glory be seen, and his disciples believed in him.

This is the Gospel of the Lord.

PAUSE

ACT OF PENITENCE

We ask forgiveness, Lord, for the irreverence and bigotry of misguided Christians. Forgive us for the times we, too, have been bigoted. Lord have mercy.

All   Lord have mercy.

Forgive us for the hurts we cause to our brothers and sisters of other denominations. Christ have mercy.

All   Christ have mercy.

We ask forgiveness for the times we have been unfaithful members of the Church. Lord have mercy.

All   Lord have mercy.

INTERCESSIONS

We pray for the unity of the body of Christ: that all may be one as Christ wills.

Let us pray for gatherings of Christians from various traditions, that they may come together in a spirit of acceptance in the search for true unity.

Lord, we pray that all married couples may grow in love for one another; that all families living in disharmony may seek an end to misunderstanding or quarrels.

Let us pray for all families broken apart; the bereaved, the separated and the divorced: may they experience Christ's presence in their difficulties.

We pray for all pilgrims to the Shrine of Our Lady of Walsingham.

Statue of Our Lady of Greeting in All Saints' Church.

Prayer at the Shrine of Our Lady of Greeting

All   Mary, you welcome us into your Son's house.
You welcome us into new life given to us in Baptism.
You welcome us to your Son's table where he feeds us with
   His body and blood.
You welcome us into the peace and joy of prayer.
Welcome us finally, most holy Mother, into the bliss of
Heaven, where with the Angels and Saints you behold the
divine splendour. AMEN

Let us meditate on the mystery of the Wedding at Cana. Jesus asked the servants to fill the stone water pots. They filled them to the brim in obedience to Mary's words: 'Do whatever He tells you.' May we obey as wholeheartedly in our quest for Christian Unity, for which intention we offer this Mystery.

Our Father ...

Third Luminous Mystery

THE PROCLAMATION OF THE KINGDOM OF GOD

Said in the Church of St Giles, Houghton St Giles

St Giles is patron saint of the disabled and those suffering from leprosy. Early Walsingham pilgrimage manuals encouraged pilgrims to visit Houghton St Giles to pray for the sick. The proclamation of God's kingdom involves preaching, healing and deliverance from the powers of darkness and evil. The Healing Ministry is one of wholeness of body, mind and spirit, and goes hand-in-hand with preaching the Word: 'And so the Lord Jesus, after he had spoken to them, was taken up into heaven: there at the right hand of God he took his place, while they, going out, preached everywhere, the Lord working with them, and confirming the word by signs that accompanied it' (Mark 16.19–20).

St Giles in stained glass in Houghton St Giles Church.

GOSPEL

Luke 4.18

The spirit of the Lord has been given to me,
for he has anointed me.
He has sent me to bring the good news to the poor,
to proclaim liberty to captives
and to the blind new sight,
to set the downtrodden free,
to proclaim the Lord's year of favour.

Mark 6.7, 12–13

(Jesus) made a tour round the villages, teaching. Then he summoned the Twelve and began to send them out in pairs, giving them authority over the unclean spirits.
So they set off to preach repentance; and they cast out many devils, and anointed many sick people with oil and cured them.

Matthew 28.18–20

(Jesus) said, 'All authority in heaven and on earth has been given to me. Go therefore, make disciples of all the nations; baptise them in the name of the Father and of the Son and of the Holy Spirit, and teach them to observe all the commands I gave you. And know that I am with you always; yes, to the end of time.'

This is the Gospel of the Lord.

PAUSE

ACT OF PENITENCE

Lord, forgive us when we are lukewarm and half-hearted in our Baptismal commitment. Lord have mercy.
All Lord have mercy.

Lord, forgive us when we doubt the ministry of Healing. Christ have mercy.
All Christ have mercy.

Lord, forgive us when we compromise with the forces of evil. Lord have mercy.
All Lord have mercy.

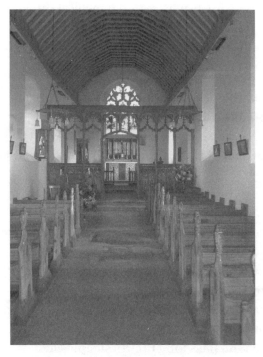

St Giles' Church interior.

INTERCESSIONS

Let us pray for the Church: that its members may be messengers of Christ's love to the world. We pray for all who do not recognise Christ as King, that they may discover Him in His followers.

Father, we pray that through prayer, laying-on of hands and anointing, the Lord's love may strengthen those who are sick.

Lord, we pray for all doctors, nurses, paramedics, pharmacists, carers and all who minister to the sick, that they may see the face of Christ in all whom they serve and continue their work with compassion and love.

Let us pray for scientists who research medical conditions and those in the pharmaceutical industry who research and develop medications and healthcare products; that they may always be motivated by the love of Christ for their fellow human beings.

We pray for all the sick, suffering and dying, especially .... May they know love, comfort and care through our active concern.

All   Mary, Health of the Sick, be at the bedside of all the world's sick;
of those who are unconscious and dying;
of those who have begun their agony;
of those who have abandoned all hope of a cure;
of those who weep and cry out in pain;
of those who cannot receive care because they have no money;
of those who ought to be resting but are forced by poverty to work;
of those who pass long nights sleeplessly;

of those who seek vainly in their beds for a less painful
position;
of those who are tormented by the cares of a family in
distress;
of those who must renounce their most cherished plans
for the future;
of those, above all, who do not believe in a better life;
of those who rebel and curse God;
of those who do not know that Christ suffered like them
and for them.
AMEN.

We offer this Mystery for all who are sick and suffering.

Our Father ...

Fourth Luminous Mystery

THE TRANSFIGURATION OF OUR LORD

Said in the Church of St Mary, Great Snoring

East Window in St Mary's Church.

'St Mary's Church in Great Snoring has commandment boards with figures representing the four last things – Death, Judgment, Heaven and Hell – flanked by the figures of Moses and Aaron' (Shell Guide to Norfolk). *These, plus its position on relatively hilly ground above Walsingham, make it an ideal place to reflect on the Transfiguration of Our Lord.*

GOSPEL   Luke 9.28–36

Jesus took with him Peter and John and James and went up the mountain to pray. As he prayed, the aspect of his face was changed and his
clothing became brilliant as lightning. Suddenly there were two men
there talking to him; they were Moses and Elijah appearing in glory,
and they were speaking of his passing which he was to accomplish in
Jerusalem. Peter and his companions were heavy with sleep, but they
kept awake and saw his glory and the two men standing with him. As
these were leaving him, Peter said to Jesus, 'Master, it is wonderful for
us to be here; so let us make three tents, one for you, one for Moses
and one for Elijah.' He did not know what he was saying. As he spoke, a
cloud came and covered them with shadow; and when they went into
the cloud, the disciples were afraid. And a voice came from the cloud,
saying, 'This is my Son, the Chosen One. Listen to him.' And after the
voice had spoken, Jesus was found alone. The disciples kept silence and,
at that time, told no one what they had seen.

This is the Gospel of the Lord.

PAUSE

ACT OF PENITENCE

Father, forgive us when we fail to respond to the light of your presence
to transform our lives. Lord have mercy.
All   Lord have mercy.

Forgive us when we refuse to take up the cross and follow you to glory.
Christ have mercy.
All   Christ have mercy.

Forgive us, Lord, when we are blind to your presence and do not allow your Holy Spirit to overshadow us. Lord have mercy.
All   Lord have mercy.

INTERCESSIONS

Father, we pray that your power may shine out in the world as it did through Jesus in His Transfiguration.

May God's people give time to listen to the voice of Jesus in this busy and noisy world.

Let us pray for those who have never known God, or who have lost faith through fear, despair or suffering; that the light of Christ's Transfiguration may shine on them and deepen their love and discipleship.

Lord, we pray for the gifts of faith, hope and trust in those promises which we cannot see; may the Transfiguration light up the dark moments of our lives, help us rise above the empty promises of the world and assure us of life after death.

We pray for all the departed; that they may be welcomed into the fuller light of Christ in their Heavenly home.

**All   Lord, teach me to seek you, and reveal yourself to me when
   I seek you,
   For I cannot seek you unless you teach me, nor find you
      except you reveal yourself.
   Let me seek you in longing, let me long for you in seeking.
   Let me find you in love and love you in finding you. AMEN**
(Prayer of St Ambrose)

Lord our God, You have made the Virgin Mary the model of all who welcome your word and who put it into practice. Open our hearts to receive it with joy and by the power of your Spirit grant that we also may become a dwelling place in which your word of salvation is fulfilled. AMEN

In the transfigured Jesus, Peter, James and John see the glory of God and the way that leads to salvation – the message of Jesus. Faith enables us, too, to come close to the Risen Christ. We pray that our faith may be deepened as we reflect upon the Transfiguration. We offer it for the intention of all who are searching for the light of faith.

Our Father …

Fifth Luminous Mystery

THE INSTITUTION OF THE EUCHARIST

Said by the altar of the Luminous Mysteries, Anglican Shrine grounds

Altar of the Luminous Mysteries, Anglican Shrine Grounds.

This altar was built in 2006 and donated by the Confraternity of the Blessed Sacrament and designed by Cooper Griffith Associates. The canopy reminds us that we are a pilgrim people on the move to the City of God. The Confraternity was founded in 1862 to pray and work for a greater devotion to Jesus Christ in the Eucharist and in the Sacrament of his Body and Blood.

READING   1 Corinthians 11.23–26

This is what I received from the Lord, and in turn passed on to you: that on the same night that he was betrayed, the Lord Jesus took some bread, and thanked God for it and broke it, and he said, 'This is my body, which is for you; do this as a memorial of me.' In the same way he took the cup after supper, and said, 'This cup is the new covenant in my blood. Whenever you drink it, do this as a memorial of me.' Until the lord comes, therefore, every time you eat this bread and drink this cup, you are proclaiming his death.

This is the Word of the Lord.

PAUSE

ACT OF PENITENCE

Forgive us, Lord, when we fail to perceive your presence in the Eucharist. Lord have mercy.
All   Lord have mercy.

Forgive us, Lord, when we come to Holy Communion ill prepared to receive you in the Blessed Sacrament. Christ have mercy.
All   Christ have mercy.

Forgive us, Lord, when we fail to serve you in our brothers and sisters. Lord have mercy.
All   Lord have mercy.

INTERCESSIONS

We pray for all who find it hard to believe in the real presence of Christ in the Eucharist.

Let us pray for the sick and housebound who receive Holy Communion from the reserved Sacrament.

Lord, we pray for those who are hungry for love; the lonely, those who are homeless, those suffering from mental health problems and those whom we find difficult to love. May our hearts be moved by compassion and love through sharing in the Eucharist.

Let us pray for all who are hungry for food: all affected by famine and disasters and for the work of all relief agencies.

Let us pray that the Eucharist may become for us the source of all our activity; for all Christians with whom we do not share our Eucharistic table, that by our common Baptism and worship of one Lord we may become one in Christ.

All   **Christ has no body now on earth but ours,**
no hands but ours,
no feet but ours.
Ours are the eyes through which Christ's compassion is to
**   look out to the earth,**
ours are the feet by which He is to go about doing good
and ours are the hands by which He is to bless us now.
                                        (From St Teresa of Avila)

Mary, give us a heart as beautiful, pure and spotless as
**   yours;**
A heart like yours, so full of love and humility.
May we be able to receive Jesus as the Bread of Life,

To love him as you loved him,
To serve him in the maltreated face of the poor.
We ask this through Jesus Christ our Lord. AMEN
(Prayer of Blessed Mother Teresa of Calcutta)

Let us meditate on the great gift of God in giving Himself to us in the Eucharist. We need this spiritual food for our Christian pilgrimage. By receiving it we have life with God now (Eternal life) and the hope of everlasting life beyond the grave.

We pray this Mystery that we may go out from Mass as the hands and feet of Christ to serve Him in our brothers and sisters throughout the world.

Our Father ...

THE SORROWFUL MYSTERIES

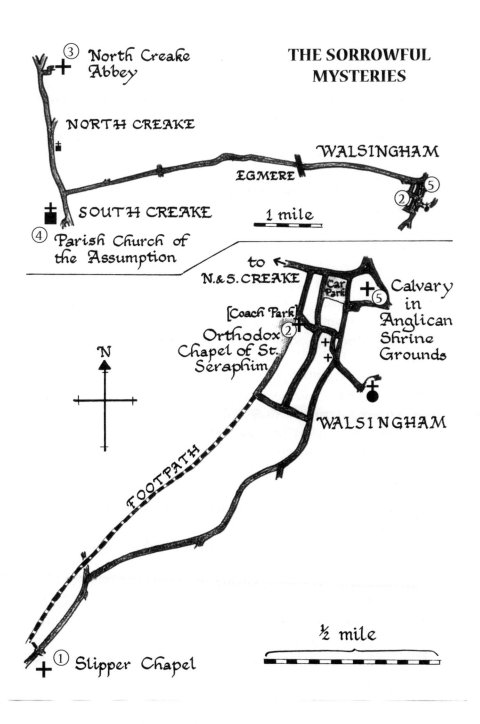

THE SORROWFUL
MYSTERIES

③ North Creake Abbey

NORTH CREAKE

WALSINGHAM

EGMERE

1 mile

⑤

② SOUTH CREAKE

④ Parish Church of the Assumption

to ← N.& S. CREAKE

Car Park

⑤ Calvary in Anglican Shrine Grounds

[Coach Park]

② Orthodox Chapel of St. Seraphim

N

WALSINGHAM

FOOTPATH

½ mile

① Slipper Chapel

DIRECTIONS

1 Slipper Chapel: RC National Shrine of Our Lady of Walsingham
There is plenty of parking by the Chapel of Reconciliation. Go through the grounds and follow signs to the Slipper Chapel. Entrance is on the left. Refreshments are available at the RC Shrine.

2 Orthodox Chapel of St Seraphim
Turn **right** out of the car park and continue along the lane with the River Stiffkey on your right.
(Walkers are encouraged to turn left just after the Shrine, then right along the hard-surfaced track of the former Fakenham-Wells railway to the Coach Park; the Orthodox Church is the former railway station on the right.)
Turn **left** after a mile at the T-junction, signed *Walsingham/Shrine OLW*, passing the ruins of the Franciscan Friary on your left. Turn **left** before the start of the High Street into Friday Market, signed *To Methodist Church.*
Turn **left** after the Black Lion into Station Road and continue up the hill, past the minor crossroads. The Orthodox Chapel is on the **left**, just before the coach park. There are a few parking spaces in front of the church and more space if you turn immediately left on the road to the coach park and park alongside the church.

3 North Creake Abbey
Turn **right** at the T-junction immediately after the Orthodox Chapel onto the approach road to the coach park.
At the T-junction turn **left**, signed *Fakenham & Wells*, and proceed along the road for one and a half miles.
At the staggered crossroads **cross over** the B1105 to Creake Road, passing the ruined Church of St Edmund, Egmere, on your left, continue for three and a half miles to a T-junction opposite a long farmhouse (the Old Black Swan).
At the T-junction turn **right** onto the B1355 to North Creake, continuing

completely through the village, passing the handsome church on your right.

About half a mile after leaving the village turn *immediately* **right** along the lane with a white picket fence at the entrance to North Creake Abbey (well signed). (**Note:** *don't take the other road diagonally to the right to Burnham Thorpe.*)

Follow the lane, bearing **left** where it forks. Park either on the green verge in front of the abbey or by the side of the approach lane. (Refreshments are available in the café in the Creake Abbey complex nearby.)

4 The Church of the Assumption of Our Lady, South Creake

Retrace your journey through North Creake, turning **left** onto the B1355 at the end of the lane, signed *Fakenham 8*. Continue through the village and into South Creake (signed). After passing a long barn conversion on your right, take next turning **right** after 40 mph sign into Church Lane, signed *Church*.

After about 200 yards the road turns sharp left, just before the church. Park by (but not on!) the verge. The church entrance is along the track behind.

5 The Calvary, Anglican Shrine grounds

Continue along Church Lane, turning **left** at the T-junction.

Turn **left** by the Old School, before the War Memorial cross on the grass triangle and **left** again onto the B1355, signed *Burnham Market 4*.

Take the next **right** after about half a mile, signed *Walsingham 5½*, continuing over the staggered crossroads after Egmere ruin and into Walsingham.

Turn **right** at the T-junction by the Anglican Shrine, to park either in the car park or Friday Market.

Walk to the Anglican Shrine grounds, past the Shrine Shop to the end of the Common Place, entering through the brick archway by the Welcome Centre. The Calvary is immediately opposite the entrance. Refreshments are available in the Norton's Café Bar in the Shrine grounds.

THE AGONY IN THE GARDEN OF GETHSEMANE

Said in the Slipper Chapel, Houghton St Giles

Slipper Chapel at the Roman Catholic Shrine.

There is a tradition that pilgrims removed their shoes in this chapel and walked the Holy Mile to Walsingham barefoot. Probably it has an older significance, for slippers and shoes are not quite synonymous. A slype is a passage-way from the cloisters to the burying ground in any ancient monastic place. The word means 'a way through' or 'something in between'. It may have been that this was the slype, or slip chapel, standing as it did between the Holy Land of Walsingham and the outer world' (H. M. Gillett, Famous Shrines of Our Lady, 1952). The mid-fourteenth-century chapel is dedicated to St Catherine of Alexandria, Patron Saint of Pilgrims and also Patroness of those who guarded the Holy Places in Palestine, including the Holy House at Nazareth. According to ancient tradition, Catherine's body was transported to Mount Sinai, the mountain of the Burning Bush, where Moses was commanded to remove his shoes before setting foot on such holy ground. So whatever the origin of 'slipper' it is still appropriate to remove shoes after the example of Moses.

GOSPEL   Luke 22.39–46

He then left the upper room to make his way as usual to the Mount of Olives, with the disciples following. When he reached the place he said to them, 'Pray not to be put to the test.'

Then he withdrew from them, about a stone's throw away, and knelt down and prayed. 'Father,' he said, 'if you are willing, take this cup away from me. Nevertheless, let your will be done, not mine.' Then an angel appeared to him, coming from heaven to give him strength. In his anguish he prayed even more earnestly, and his sweat fell to the ground like great drops of blood.

When he rose from prayer he went to the disciples and found them sleeping for sheer grief. And he said to them, 'Why are you asleep? Get up and pray not to be put to the test.'

This is the Gospel of the Lord.

PAUSE

ACT OF PENITENCE

Forgive us, Lord, when we have failed to live up to your words: 'Let your will be done, not mine'. Forgive us for our failure to see that prayer gives us strength from God. Lord have mercy.
All   Lord have mercy.

Forgive us, Lord, when we have been guilty of betrayal; when we have been overcome by the betrayal of our friends; when we have not dared to acknowledge you as Lord. Christ have mercy.
All   Christ have mercy.

Forgive us, Lord, for our failure to share in the agony and pain of other people; for our failure to respond to the lonely or to those who face death, famine, violence and oppression. Lord have mercy.
All   Lord have mercy.

INTERCESSION

Let us pray for all facing a great crisis, especially the lonely and those who cannot conquer their fear of death.

Lord, we pray for all who are experiencing anguish or distress; those diagnosed with a serious or terminal illness; anyone struggling with mental or emotional sickness; those crushed by failure.

We pray for all who have been let down or betrayed by their friends.

We pray that when we experience something of Gethsemane we may be given God's grace to bear it, placing our wills in union with His in all things.

All   **Remember, O most gracious Virgin Mary, that never was it known that anyone who fled to thy protection, implored thy help, or sought thy intercession was left unaided, Inspired by this confidence I fly unto thee, O virgin of virgins, my Mother. To thee do I come, before thee I stand, sinful and sorrowful. O Mother of the Word Incarnate, despise not my petitions, but in thy mercy, hear and answer me. AMEN**

(St Bernard of Clairvaux)

Let us pray for a deeper understanding of suffering, loneliness, failure and death. Jesus deliberately missed His chances for worldly success and chose instead failure for our salvation.

We pray this Mystery for all suffering and lonely people, especially those suffering from addictions and those viewed by themselves or others as failures.

Our Father ...

Second Sorrowful Mystery

THE SCOURGING OF OUR LORD

Said in the Orthodox Chapel of St Seraphim, Little Walsingham

Orthodox Chapel of St Seraphim.

This must surely be the only instance of conversion of a station house into a Russian Orthodox Church. Services are held in what was the booking hall. This church was blessed by the Russian Archbishop Nikodem in 1967. It is a custom upon entering an Orthodox church to venerate the Ikons of the Saviour, the Mother of God and the Patron Saint. St Seraphim of Sarov was born in Kurst in 1759 and died at Sarov in 1833. He was the son of a builder and at the age of 20 entered the monastery of Sarov, where he took the name of Seraphim. He was ordained priest in 1793. He lived the life of a hermit and it is said that several times during his life he experienced visions of the Blessed Virgin Mary.

GOSPEL   Matthew 27.20–26

The chief priests and the elders had persuaded the crowd to demand the release of Barabbas and the execution of Jesus. So when the governor asked them, 'Which of the two do you want me to release for you?' they said, 'Barabbas.' 'But in that case,' Pilate said to them, 'what am I to do with Jesus who is called Christ?' They all said, 'Let him be crucified!' 'Why?' he asked, 'What harm has he done?' But they shouted all the louder, 'Let him be crucified!' Then Pilate saw that he was making no impression, that in fact a riot was imminent. So he took some water, washed his hands in front of the crowd and said, 'I am innocent of this man's blood. It is your concern.' And the people, to a man, shouted back, 'His blood be on us and on our children!' Then he released Barabbas for them. He ordered Jesus to be first scourged and then handed over to be crucified.

This is the Gospel of the Lord.

PAUSE

ACT OF PENITENCE

Forgive us, Lord, when we are like Pilate and abdicate our responsibilities; when we ignore injustices in our own communities; when we turn a blind eye to problems in the world. Lord have mercy.

All   Lord have mercy.

Forgive us, Lord, when like the Pharisees we fuss over trivialities but do not mind punishing and crucifying others. Christ have mercy.

All   Christ have mercy.

Forgive us, Lord, when, like Judas, we have doubted your mercy and despaired of your forgiveness by thinking our sins too great for your mercy and absolution. Lord have mercy.

All Lord have mercy.

Ikon of Christ in the Orthodox Chapel.

INTERCESSIONS

Let us pray that we may have strength, when in physical pain, to face it and treat it as one lash of Christ's scourging.

We pray for all who are condemned to death and all who take any part in carrying out a death sentence; for all prisoners and captives and all tortured by the memory of the pain they have inflicted.

Lord, we pray for those who have lost control over their lives; the elderly who are unable to look after themselves; those without work; those in prison and all who care for them.

Let us pray for all who are tortured because of their faith in Christ.

Father, we pray for all victims of physical abuse, crime and war; for all who lack food and water.

We pray for all the people we have hurt through our pride, jealousies, false and unkind words; may we be given the grace to heal their broken hearts.

Lord, we pray for the Eastern Orthodox Patriarchs, the Metropolitans of the Eastern Orthodox Churches in Great Britain and the clergy, religious and laity.

All   Father in Heaven, You changed Mary's sorrow into joy at the Resurrection of your Son; grant to those who suffer the grace and peace of Your Holy Spirit, who is Lord for ever and ever. AMEN

Let us meditate on the scourging. The Pharisees would not enter the palace, because it would make them legally 'unclean'; yet while they fussed about trivialities, they did not mind crucifying Christ.

Let us pray this Mystery for all who govern and for all people who suffer under oppressive regimes.

Our Father ...

THE CROWNING WITH THORNS

Said at North Creake Abbey

All that remains of the abbey are parts of the transepts, crossings, choir and chapels. The abbey was founded in 1206 by Sir Robert de Narford, Governor of Dover Castle, and his wife, Alice, as a hospital and church dedicated to St Bartholomew, for a master, four chaplains and 13 lay brethren. The first master soon became a prior of the Order of St Augustine and the community became affiliated to the Augustinian Order in 1227. In 1231 Henry III raised its status to an abbey. In 1484 a disastrous fire destroyed the nave and transepts, then followed a plague which killed all except the abbot. He died alone in 1506, at which point the revenues reverted to the Crown. These were diverted to Christ's College, Cambridge. This abbey was not dissolved by Henry VIII.

———————

GOSPEL   Matthew 27.27–31

Then the governor's soldiers took Jesus with them into the Praetorium and collected the whole cohort round him. And they stripped him and put a scarlet cloak round him, and having twisted some thorns into a crown they put this on his head and placed a reed in his right hand. To make fun of him they knelt to him saying, 'Hail, king of the Jews!' And they spat on him and took the reed and struck him on the head with it. And when they had finished making fun of him, they took off the cloak and dressed him in his own clothes and led him away to crucify him.

This is the Gospel of the Lord.

North Creake Abbey.

PAUSE

ACT OF PENITENCE

Forgive us, Lord, when we have sought earthly crowns. Lord have mercy.
All   Lord have mercy.

Forgive us, Lord, for the times we have mocked and ridiculed other people. Christ have mercy.
All   Christ have mercy.

Forgive us, Lord, when our silence and inaction have misled or offended other people. Lord have mercy.
All   Lord have mercy.

INTERCESSIONS

Father, we pray for all who are bearing the burden of failure; for all who have failed exams or failed in their business; for all who are unemployed; for all betrayed by friends.

Let us pray for all who are victims of persecution or who are stripped of their dignity; for all who are falsely accused; for all subjected to emotional abuse.

Lord, we pray for all who hold the sceptre of any kind of power; for all who misuse authority and become corrupted by power; for all who plan and carry out evil.

We pray for all unjustly mocked; for those struggling to keep to Christian standards; for all victims of domestic violence, or racial and religious hatred.

Let us pray for all who are sick, that through the Laying on of hands, Anointing and Prayer, the Lord's love may strengthen and heal them.

Father, we pray for all who have consecrated themselves in the religious life; that their capacity to love and be loved might be enhanced in lives of prayer and service.

Prayer to the Mother of Good Counsel
(As used in the Augustinian Priory at Clare, Suffolk)

All   Mary, our Mother, we thank you that we can always call upon you to help us in our need. You were chosen from the whole human race and entrusted by God, Creator of the universe, to nurture His Son, Jesus, and to guide His steps. It is with confidence that we come to you now and, pondering on how you held Jesus in your heart and in your arms, we ask you to hold us in the same way, so that we can be close to you and to your Son. Show us how to reveal Jesus to others with gentleness and love and guide us with wisdom and good counsel on our journey through life. AMEN

Let us meditate on the mystery of the Crowning with Thorns. Judas was guilty and destroyed himself, but Peter was penitent and was restored in Christ.

We pray this Mystery that we may be more penitent people and experience Christ's renewal and reconciliation.

Our Father ...

Fourth Sorrowful Mystery

THE CARRYING OF THE CROSS

Said at the Church of the Assumption of Our Lady, South Creake

Mediaeval glass depicting the Crucifixion in the Church of the Assumption of Our Lady.

'This wonderful church is in many ways the finest in Norfolk; it has the atmosphere of a very holy place, a sense of timelessness' (W. Harrod, Shell Guide to Norfolk, 1982). 'With its spacious nave, St Mary's South Creake shows, better than any other church in Norfolk, what a great building of this sort would have looked like in the fifteenth century' (W. Harrod and C. L. S. Linnell, Shell Guide to Norfolk, 1958). 'This beautiful parish church has been most wonderfully restored and is a model for all ancient parish churches. Make a visit here to pray for the conversion of England and for restoration of Catholic worship in all the churches in our land' (Walsingham Pilgrims' Manual, 1960).

GOSPEL   Matthew 27.32–38

On their way out, they came across a man from Cyrene, called Simon, and enlisted him to carry his cross. When they had reached a place called Golgotha, that is, the place of the skull, they gave him wine to drink mixed with gall, which he tasted but refused to drink. When they had finished crucifying him they shared out his clothing by casting lots, and then sat down and stayed there keeping guard over him.

Above his head was placed the charge against him; it read: 'This is Jesus, the King of the Jews.' At the same time two robbers were crucified with him, one on the right and one on the left.

This is the Gospel of the Lord.

PAUSE

ACT OF PENITENCE

Lord, forgive us for the times we fail to help carry other people's burdens. Lord have mercy.
All   Lord have mercy.

Lord, forgive us for passing judgements on others; forgive us when we condemn others because of the company they keep, or for their lifestyle, or for their political adherence. Christ have mercy.
All   Christ have mercy.

Lord, forgive us for the times we have failed to comfort those in need because we did not listen. Lord have mercy.
All   Lord have mercy.

INTERCESSIONS

We pray for those with drug and alcohol dependencies, for prostitutes and those who care for them.

Let us pray for all people who are victims of HIV and AIDS, particularly those rejected by families and friends.

Lord, we pray for victims of natural disasters, fire or flood; for those whose lives have been ruined by violence or terrorism.

Father, may we become more aware of the sufferings of others. Let us remember those who, like Simon of Cyrene, help carry other people's burdens; for relief workers in those areas of the world suffering from natural disasters or the aftermath of war; for employment agencies trying to find work for those without any.

Let us pray for ourselves; that we may not be concerned with being respectable, but will carry the cross of Jesus as far as the Place of the Skull.

Angel roof boss.

All   **O Holy Virgin, in the midst of your days of glory, do not forget the sorrows of this earth. Cast a merciful glance upon those who are suffering, struggling against difficulties, with their lips constantly pressed against life's bitter cup. Have pity on those who love each other and are separated. Have pity on our rebellious hearts; Have pity on our weak faith; Have pity on those we love; Have pity on those who weep, on those who pray, on those who fear. Grant hope and peace to all. AMEN**

(Abbé Perryve)

Let us meditate on the fourth Sorrowful Mystery, which teaches us perseverance, for Christ struggled on in spite of pain, hunger, thirst and fatigue. Simon of Cyrene carried the Cross and we imitate him every time we shoulder someone's burden.

Let us pray this Mystery for victims of natural disasters, violence or terrorism.

Our Father ...

Fifth Sorrowful Mystery

THE CRUCIFIXION

Said in the grounds of the Anglican Shrine on the Hill of Calvary

---

GOSPEL   Luke 23: 33–46

When they reached the place called The Skull, there they crucified him and the other two criminals, one on his right and the other on his left. Jesus said, 'Father, forgive them; they do not know what they are doing.' Then they cast lots to share out his clothing.

The people stayed there watching. As for the leaders, they jeered at him with the words, 'He saved others, let him save himself if he is the Christ of God, the chosen One.' The soldiers mocked him too, coming up to him, offering him vinegar and saying, 'If you are the king of the Jews, save yourself.' Above him there was an inscription: 'This is the King of the Jews'.

One of the criminals hanging there abused him: 'Are you the Christ? Save yourself and us as well.' But the other spoke up and rebuked him. 'Have you no fear of God at all?' he said. 'You got the same sentence as he did, but in our case we deserved it: we are paying for what we did. But this man has done nothing wrong.' Then he said, 'Jesus, remember me when you come into your kingdom.' He answered him, 'In truth I tell you, today you will be with me in paradise.'

It was now about the sixth hour and, with the sun eclipsed, a darkness came over the whole land until the ninth hour. The veil of the sanctuary was torn right down the middle. Jesus cried out in a loud voice saying, 'Father, into your hands I commit my spirit.' With these words he breathed his last.

This is the Gospel of the Lord.

PAUSE

ACT OF PENITENCE

Lord, forgive us when we fail to give ourselves to you. Lord have mercy.
All   Lord have mercy.

Lord, forgive us for the times we fail to forgive others; when we crucify them. Christ have mercy.
All   Christ have mercy.

The Hill of Calvary in the Anglican Shrine grounds.

Lord, forgive us for the times we turn our backs on victims of war; on broken families; on the unemployed and homeless. Lord have mercy.
All   Lord have mercy.

INTERCESSIONS

Let us pray for the dying: for those who have terminal illness; for all who feel forsaken and afraid; for those in the darkness of despair; for all being absolved today.

We pray for all parents who see their children die; for all concerned with the dying and bereaved, especially nurses, doctors, undertakers, registrars and priests, that they may find words and actions that are truly comforting.

Let us pray forgiveness for those who do not respect human life; for proper support and counselling for all mothers facing problem pregnancies, and that doctors, nurses and social workers will look after them and their unborn and newly born babies with true compassion and devotion.

Father, we pray for all who have been deprived of love of family and friends; for all who cannot have a family; for all families living in disharmony because of misunderstanding or quarrels.

We pray for the dead. Jesus said to the penitent thief, 'Truly I say to you, this day you will be with me in Paradise.' May these words be heard by our departed brothers and sisters.

All **Father, as your Son was raised on the cross, His mother Mary stood by Him, sharing his sufferings. May your Church be united with Christ in His suffering and death and so come to share in His rising to new life, where He lives and reigns for ever and ever. AMEN**

Let us meditate on suffering, death and forgiveness. Jesus forgave His enemies. Many people carry burdens of revenge and resentment because they are unable to forgive. We pray that we may all find in Christ's example the ability to forgive and experience peace of heart and mind.

We pray this Mystery for the intention of the dead – our departed relatives and friends and those who have no-one to pray for them.

Our Father ...

THE GLORIOUS MYSTERIES

THE GLORIOUS MYSTERIES

GREAT WALSINGHAM

① Parish Church of St. Peter

Guild of ② All Souls Chapel

LITTLE WALSINGHAM

Coach Park

③ + Walsingham Abbey (Priory ruins)

N

FOOTPATH

½ mile

HOUGHTON ST. GILES

⑤ Chapel of Reconciliation +

Parish ④ + Church of All Saints

NORTH BARSHAM

DIRECTIONS

1 St Peter's Church, Great Walsingham

From the Pump near the Shrine Shop in the centre of Little Walsingham, go past the Bull and turn **left** immediately after the Anglican Shrine into Knight Street, signed *Fakenham 5, Wells 5, Wighton 2*. Continue along the Wells Road, past the War Memorial on the left. Turn at the next **right** after the Recreation Ground into St Peter's Road (school on corner). St Peter's Church is about a quarter of a mile on the **left**, after a row of bungalows/chalets. Turn diagonally **left**, up a steep grassy incline just before two triangular road signs into a field in front of the church and park.

2 Chantry Chapel of St Michael and the Holy Souls

Retrace the last journey, turning **right** out of the parking area, and return to the T-junction by the school, then turn **left** past the War Memorial towards the Anglican Shrine.

Turn **right** at the T-junction by the Anglican Shrine to park either in the car park past the Pump or in Friday Market.

Walk back past the Shrine Shop to the Anglican Shrine on the left of Common Place. Turn **left** through the brick archway and **right** into the Shrine grounds. The Guild of All Souls Chapel is the red brick octagonal chapel in the grounds, immediately before the steps down to the Shrine. Refreshments are available in the Norton's Café Bar in the Shrine grounds.

3 Walsingham Abbey grounds

Walk through the *'Brandie arch'*, turning **right** into Common Place, crossing the road to pass the Bull on your left to the Tourist Information Centre. The abbey grounds are normally entered here. Opening times are 11.00am–4.00pm (there is an admission charge). When the museum is closed, entry is through the estate office to the left at the corner of the buildings.

Once in the grounds, proceed towards the large grassy area, dominated by the great arch. The site of the Lady Chapel is nearby in the grass towards the main gateway, and marked with a wooden cross. Refreshments are available at the Bull and the Black Lion.

4 All Saints' Church, North Barsham

Walking – Turn **left** along the High Street and take the first **right** into Friday Market, signed *Orthodox Church*. Continue past the Black Lion on your left, up Station Road, and take the first **left** at the small crossroads into Back Lane to walk along the narrow lane behind the RC Pilgrim Bureau and the Friary ruins. Turn **right** at the T-junction at the end of Back Lane into a very narrow lane *(look out for coaches)* for about 50 yards, then turn first **left** along the track of a former railway – a designated walk which has a good surface.

Continue for about three-quarters of a mile until the hard surface stops, near Slipper Chapel, turning **left** into a track, then **right** into a road. Walk on the right side of the road (passing the Slipper Chapel and Chapel of Reconciliation on the left) for a further half a mile (looking out for traffic). After a right bend, the road bears sharp left by a large house (the former Rectory); turn **right** here up the grassy track to North Barsham Church.

Driving – Leave Walsingham by the High Street towards Fakenham (passing the Friary ruins and a lane to the coach park on your right) and turn on the next **right** towards the RC Shrine, signed *N&W Barsham, Slipper Chapel and Shrine* where the road bends left for Fakenham.

Continue for about two miles, passing the RC Shrine on the left and then the abutments of a disused railway bridge, after which North Barsham Church comes into view on the right.

After the road bends right, prepare for the next sharp bend to the left by a large house (the former Rectory), where you turn **right** into a grassy track leading to the church. Park beyond the entrance to the house.

5 Chapel of Reconciliation, RC Shrine

Retrace your journey, turning **left** out of the track and going as far as the car park of the RC Shrine, half a mile on the **right**. The Chapel of Reconciliation is the large building immediately by the car park, built in the style of a Norfolk barn. The entrance is well marked. Refreshments are available at the RC Shrine.

First Glorious Mystery

THE RESURRECTION

Said in the Parish Church of St Peter, Great Walsingham

St Peter's Church.

'This is a homogeneous and beautiful Decorated Church, having lovely window tracery, benches with poppyheads and carved backs and some fourteenth century Norwich glass' (W. Harrod and C. L. S. Linnell, Collins' Guide to Parish Churches of England and Wales).'A warm, friendly church, its charm grows on you the longer you stay in it' (J. J. Norwich, The Architecture of Southern England, 1985). There is a beautiful fragment of mediaeval glass at the top of the second window from the East end of the North aisle which depicts the risen Christ. Also, on the carved poppyhead at the end of the fourth pew from the East end of the Nave is a mediaeval carving believed to be of Our Lady of Walsingham, but sadly defaced by seventeenth-century iconoclasts.

GOSPEL   Luke 24.35-48

The disciples told their story of what had happened on the road and how they had recognised Jesus at the breaking of bread.

They were still talking about all this when Jesus himself stood among them and said to them, 'Peace be with you!' In a state of alarm and fright, they thought they were seeing a ghost. But he said, 'Why are you so agitated, and why are these doubts rising in your hearts? Look at my hands and feet; yes, it is I indeed. Touch me and see for yourselves; a ghost has no flesh and bones as you can see I have.' And as he said this he showed them his hands and feet. Their joy was so great that they still could not believe it, and they stood there dumbfounded; so he said to them, 'Have you anything here to eat?' and they offered him a piece of grilled fish, which he took and ate before their eyes.

Then he told them, 'This is what I meant when I said, while I was still with you, that everything written about me in the Law of Moses, in the Prophets and in the Psalms has to be fulfilled.' He then opened their minds to understand the scriptures, and he said to them, 'So you see how it is written that the Christ would suffer and on the third day rise from the dead, and that, in his name, repentance for the forgiveness of sins would be preached to all the nations, beginning from Jerusalem. You are witnesses to this.'

This is the Gospel of the Lord.

PAUSE

85

ACT OF PENITENCE

Forgive us, Lord, when, like the apostles, we have been locked up in our own fears and have lacked faith. Lord have mercy.

All **Lord have mercy.**

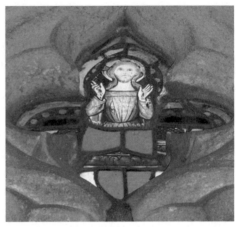

Forgive us, Lord, when we have been depressed and lonely, agitated and afraid. Christ have mercy.

All **Christ have mercy.**

Mediaeval glass depicting the Resurrection in St Peter's Church.

Forgive us, Lord, for our lack of fervour and enthusiasm in Christian witness. Lord have mercy.

All **Lord have mercy.**

INTERCESSIONS

Let us pray that we may remove all stones from our hearts and respond promptly and wholeheartedly in obeying God's will.

We pray that we may be a more dedicated people of God. The anointing of Christ's body reminds us of our anointing with Chrism at Baptism and Confirmation and of priests at Ordination. May we respond whole-heartedly to our vocation.

We give thanks, Lord, for the Sacrament of Holy Baptism and for parents, godparents and sponsors. Help us to renew our commitment now, so that Jesus may continue to work through each one of us.

Let us pray for more vocations to the priesthood, that the Lord will call men who will speak to people with courage and conviction.

Let us pray for the Pope, successor of St Peter and for the unity of all Christians.

Father, we pray that something of Christ's glory may be seen in us in our daily lives.

All   **Hail Mary, full of grace; all generations will call you blessed.**
Hail, Mother of God; when asked by the angel to bear the Son of the Most High, filled with faith, you responded, 'Let it be done unto me.'
Holy Mother of Jesus, at the wedding feast at Cana you prompted your Son to perform His first sign. Be with us as we discern our life's work and guide us in the way we are called, to follow in the footsteps of your Son.
Holy Mother of the Good Shepherd, turn your motherly care to this nation. Intercede for us to the Lord of the harvest in this land dedicated to your honour.
Queen of Peace, Mirror of Justice, Health of the Sick, inspire vocations in our time. Let the word of your Son be made flesh anew in the lives of people anxious to proclaim the good news of everlasting life. AMEN

As we meditate on the Mystery of the Resurrection let us pray that we may remove any stone that prevents us from being God's Easter people.

We offer it for the intention of vocations to the priesthood, for ordinands, for clergy and for a more committed laity.

Our Father ...

Second Glorious Mystery

THE ASCENSION OF OUR LORD

Said in the Guild of All Souls Chapel in the Anglican Shrine grounds

The Guild of All Souls Chapel in the Anglican Shrine grounds.

The foundation stone for this chapel, dedicated to St Michael and All Souls, was laid in 1965 by the Bishop of Exeter and it was consecrated by the Bishop of Fond du Lac. Designed by Laurence King, this is the chantry chapel of the Guild of All Souls, which was founded in 1873. The Guild's mission is to pray and care for the sick, dying, departed and bereaved.

GOSPEL   Luke 24.49–53

'And now I am sending upon you what the Father promised. Stay in the city, then, until you are clothed with the power from on high.'

Then he took them out as far as the outskirts of Bethany, and lifting up his hands he blessed them. Now as he blessed them, he withdrew from them and was carried up to heaven. They worshipped him and then went back to Jerusalem full of joy; and they were continually in the temple praising God.

This is the Gospel of the Lord.

PAUSE

ACT OF PENITENCE

In Your Ascension, Lord, you show us the way to share your glory. Forgive us when we allow the attractions of this world to dim our vision. Lord have mercy.
All   Lord have mercy.

At Your Ascension, Lord, you said: 'Stay in the city until you are clothed with power from on high'. Forgive us when we have allowed activity and noise to prevent the power of the Holy Spirit from overshadowing our lives. Christ have mercy.
All   Christ have mercy.

After Your Ascension, Lord, the disciples went back to Jerusalem full of joy. Forgive us for failing to be joyful Christian people. Lord have mercy.
All   Lord have mercy.

INTERCESSIONS

We pray for grace to proclaim the Good News by reflecting Jesus to others; may we never lose courage, but be witnesses for Christ to the ends of the earth.

'This same Jesus will come back in the same way as you have seen Him go there.' Let us pray that we may wait in joyful hope for the coming of Jesus in glory.

Lord, we pray that, by the power of His Ascension, Christ may deliver us from all evil and help us to live our faith joyfully.

Let us pray for all the bereaved, especially those suffering from distress, guilt, lack of forgiveness, sleeplessness, depression, loneliness, anger or lack of purpose; may they experience the love of Christ.

We pray for all the dead – especially those commemorated in this chantry chapel. May they experience the joys of Heaven in the company of all the saints.

Crucifix in the Guild of All Souls Chapel.

All **Holy Michael Archangel, defend us in the day of battle; be our safeguard against the wickedness and snares of the devil. May God rebuke him, we humbly pray; and do thou, prince of the Heavenly host, by the power of God, thrust down to Hell Satan and all wicked spirits, who wander through the world for the ruin of souls. AMEN**

Let us meditate on the Ascension of our Lord. It was a mystery of joy and an opportunity to prepare for the Holy Spirit; it points to Christ's coming in glory and reminds us that, until He comes again, we are His hands and feet in the world.

We offer this Mystery for the Unity of all God's people.

Our Father ...

Third Glorious Mystery

THE COMING OF THE HOLY SPIRIT

Said on the site of the Lady Chapel in the grounds of
Walsingham Abbey

The Abbey, in private ownership, is the site of a former Augustinian Priory. It was founded by Geoffrey de Faverches (son of Richeldis, who received the vision of Our Lady) in 1153. Of the remains the most impressive is the East wall of the church, with a very large window and two turrets. The original main gate is in the High Street, a fifteenth-century building with the carved head of a porter looking for pilgrims. Opposite the gateway is the Martyr's house, where Nicholas Myleham was detained before his execution on

East Wall of Walsingham Abbey.

Martyr's Hill in 1538. He was the sub-prior, who resisted Henry VIII's suppression of the monasteries.

Behind the East window of the priory are the twin wells and site of St Lawrence's Chapel.

READING   Acts 2.1–4

When Pentecost came round, the apostles had all met in one room, when suddenly they heard what sounded like a powerful wind from heaven, the noise of which filled the entire house in which they were sitting; and something appeared to them that seemed like tongues of fire; these separated and came to rest on the head of each of them. They were all filled with the Holy Spirit and began to speak different languages as the Spirit gave them power to express themselves.

This is the Word of the Lord.

PAUSE

ACT OF PENITENCE

Lord, forgive us for our failure to see your active presence in our lives. Lord have mercy.

All   Lord have mercy.

Lord, forgive us for our failure to make friendships and be united with one another. Christ have mercy.

All   Christ have mercy.

Lord, forgive us when we have not been open to the Holy Spirit to heal the wounds of division in our Christian communities. Lord have mercy.

All   Lord have mercy.

INTERCESSIONS

Let us pray that we may follow Mary's attitude of openness to risk and to trust in the Holy Spirit's power.

Father, we pray for all those who are imprisoned by fears, doubts, loneliness, depression or habitual sin; that the Holy Spirit may set them free.

Lord, we pray that within our local communities we may live in closer harmony with one another through the Holy Spirit and be effective witnesses for Christ in our daily lives.

We pray for all terrorists, that the Spirit of peace may touch their hearts. May He turn them from violence and lead them to gentleness and self-control.

We pray that Christians will work to eliminate the scandal of disunity as we are all called to be parts of one body united in Jesus Christ.

Let us pray for all who are persecuted for their faith; for those in prison because their human rights have been violated and for those who cannot practise their faith.

All   Give me strength to seek You, Lord, for you have already enabled me to find you and have given me hope of finding you ever more fully. AMEN

(St Augustine)

O God, your martyrs give us a wonderful example of courage, loyalty and faith. Grant that through the intercession of those who died for the unity of the Church, all Christians may be inspired by their witness to the truth and strive to bring about the unity of all believers as willed by the Father. We make this prayer through Christ our Lord. AMEN

We offer this Mystery for all preparing for Baptism and Confirmation, and that we may be more open to the Holy Spirit.

Our Father ...

THE ASSUMPTION OF MARY INTO HEAVEN

Said in the Church of All Saints, North Barsham

Church of All Saints.

This is a small church consisting of a nave and chancel. It contains a monument to Philip Russell, who 'spunne out his thred of time, in ye dimention of 66 yeares, whereof ye last 36 ran smoothly in ye Bonde of Marriage with Kathren …' and whose 'exanimated body' went to 'ye common mother of us all' in December 1617. There used to be a chapel here dedicated to St Catherine in 1531, but all traces have disappeared.

READING   1 Corinthians 15.20–23

Christ has been raised from the dead, the first-fruits of all who have fallen asleep. Death came through one man and in the same way the resurrection of the dead has come through one man. Just as all men die in Adam, so all men will be brought to life in Christ; but all of them in their proper order: Christ as the first-fruits and then, after the coming of Christ, those who belong to him.

> This is the Word of the Lord.

PAUSE

ACT OF PENITENCE

Forgive us, Lord, when we do our will rather than yours. Lord have mercy.

All   Lord have mercy.

Forgive us, Lord, when we are selfish and are not open to you. Christ have mercy.

All   Christ have mercy.

Forgive us when we are half-hearted in our Christian commitment. Lord have mercy.

All   Lord have mercy.

INTERCESSIONS

Mary's Assumption is her glorification in Heaven. She now shares fully in the Easter victory that Christ her Son gained over death. Let us realise afresh that we, too, are called to glory in body, mind and spirit.

Mary's Assumption brings home to us the thought of death. Each night the Church's prayer is: 'May the Lord grant us a quiet night and a perfect end.' Let us pray that we may be delivered from sudden and unprepared death and for hope and confidence at the moment of our death.

We pray for the dying; for those dying in pain; for those dying alone and unloved; for those dying with little or no faith and for those dying receiving the last rites of the Church.

Let us pray for a greater respect and care of our bodies; that we may reverence them as temples of the Holy Spirit, who will do great things for us if we are open to Him.

Father, we pray for those caring for the terminally ill, particularly our local hospices and Macmillan nurses and for all whose work brings them close to the mystery of death.

Lord, may we always show reverence and care for the churchyards and cemeteries where our dead rest in hope of Resurrection. May our care for these consecrated places reflect our own faith in the Resurrection of the body and everlasting life.

All   Father, Mary was full of grace at all times, from the very beginning of her life until the last moment. May she be with us at every moment of our lives: in calm and troubled moments and at the hour of our death, so that that moment may become the moment of our glory. We ask this through Christ our Lord. AMEN

Let us meditate on Mary's Assumption into Heaven in body and soul. This Mystery calls us to reflect on death and to appreciate the holiness of our bodies which, in their risen glory, will endure for ever. We offer it for the intention of the dying.

Our Father ...

Fifth Glorious Mystery

THE CORONATION OF MARY AS QUEEN OF HEAVEN

Said in the Chapel of Reconciliation, RC Shrine (dedicated 1982)

'Very beautiful, this new church, as captivating in its simplicity as in its purpose, as it nestles a great barn of a house of prayer and praise amid the solitude and beauty of its Norfolk countryside. Because it is new and full of promise for the future it figures in the next chapter, the hope, the longing of so many hearts is that it may bear a great part in the reconciliation, the unity of all Christians, not only of the Churches but of all mankind' (Claude Fisher, Walsingham, A Place of Pilgrimage for All People, *1983*).

The Ikon of Our Lady of Walsingham to the left of the altar was a gift from the Orthodox Church. The theme of

Ikon of Our Lady of Walsingham in the Chapel of Reconciliation.

reconciliation and Christian Unity is one which brings Christians to Walsingham that it may be a centre for all Christians to unite in their love of Jesus and His mother Mary.

The Mystery of the Coronation of Our Lady as Queen of Heaven is said before the Ikon.

98

READING

Revelation 7.9–10, 11.19–12.1

After that I saw a huge number, impossible to count, of people from every nation, race, tribe and language; they were standing in front of the throne and in front of the Lamb, dressed in white robes and holding palms in their hands. They shouted aloud, 'Victory to our God, who sits on the throne, and to the Lamb!'

Then the sanctuary of God in heaven opened, and the Ark of the Covenant could be seen inside it. Then came flashes of lightning, peals of thunder and an earthquake, and violent hail. Now a great sign appeared in heaven: a woman, adorned with the sun, standing on the moon, and with twelve stars on her head for a crown.

1 Corinthians 9.24–25

All the runners at the stadium are trying to win, but only one of them gets the prize. You must run in the same way, meaning to win. All the fighters at the games go into strict training; they do this just to win a wreath that will wither away, but we do it for a wreath that will never wither.

This is the Word of the Lord.

PAUSE

ACT OF PENITENCE

Forgive us, Lord, for the quarrels in our families, communities and Church which we do not attempt to mend. Lord have mercy.
All   Lord have mercy.

Forgive us, Lord, for those times we are afraid to let go of this life. Christ have mercy.
All   Christ have mercy.

Forgive us, Lord, when we feel neglected and depressed and our trust in your goodness seems to fail. Lord have mercy.
All   Lord have mercy.

INTERCESSIONS

Let us pray for all who love and honour Blessed Mary; for all societies that promote her honour.

We pray for churches and shrines throughout Christendom that are dedicated to her honour. May those who visit them as pilgrims and tourists have their hearts uplifted and realise something of the beauty of God's glory.

Father, may we rejoice in our royal priesthood as the Baptised and experience Mary's protection and prayers in our Christian pilgrimage.

Let us pray for a deeper commitment to spiritual growth and holiness; that we, too, may come to the glories of Heaven and share with Mary the crown of life.

In this Chapel of Reconciliation let us pray for a new heart and a new spirit, that we may live in harmony with one another as God's people. We await with joy the day when we shall be perfectly one, so the world may know that You, Father, have sent Your Son Jesus to redeem us.

View across fields to the Chapel of Reconciliation in the Roman Catholic National Shrine.

All   Mary, my Mother, pray for me that I may one day share in your joy and see the Father in all His glory. AMEN

O Unfailing Intercessor of Christians, O Constant Mediatress before the Creator, despise not the cry of us sinners, but of thy goodness, come speedily to the help of us who in faith call upon thee. Hasten to offer swift intercession and prayer for us, O Mother of God, who ever intercedest for those who honour thee. More honourable than the Cherubim and incomparably more glorious than the Seraphim, thou who in virginity didst bear God the Word, thee, true Mother of God, we magnify. AMEN

(Orthodox prayer)

Let us meditate on the Coronation of Mary, reflecting on how things ought to be on earth and how they are in Heaven. Mary is the model of what we hope to be. In the Lord's Prayer we pray: 'Thy kingdom come. Thy will be done on earth as it is in Heaven.' We ask that we may know and do God's will. Mary has always done this and we pray this Mystery for the Peace of the World.

Our Father ...